Editor
Mara Ellen Guckian

Editorial Project Manager
Ina Massler Levin, M.A.

Editor in Chief
Sharon Coan, M.S. Ed.

Illustrator
Andi Tanner

Cover Artist
Sue Fullam

Art Coordinator
Denice Adorno

Creative Director
Elayne Roberts

Imaging
Ralph Olmedo, Jr.

Product Manager
Phil Garcia

Acknowledgements
KidPix® is a registered
trademark of The Learning
Company.
ClarisWorks® is a registered
trademark of Apple Corporation.
HyperStudio® is a registered
trademark of Roger Wagner
Publishing, Inc.
*Microsoft Encarta 97
Encyclopedia*® is a registered
trademark of the Microsoft
Corporation.

Publishers
Rachelle Cracchiolo, M.S. Ed.
Mary Dupuy Smith, M.S. Ed.

How a Simple Report

Grades 1–3

Author

Jennifer Overend Prior, M.Ed.

Teacher Created Materials, Inc.
6421 Industry Way
Westminster, CA 92683
www.teachercreated.com
ISBN-1-57690-502-0
©1999 Teacher Created Materials, Inc.
Made in U.S.A.

Table of Contents

Introduction 3

Getting Started 4

What is a Report?   Thinking About Your Topic
Write a Class Report   The Five Ws
Let's Get Specific!

Using the Library 11

The Dewey Decimal System   Where Can I Find It?
Searching for Books   Using a CD-ROM Encyclopedia
Finding Books on Library Shelves   Searching the Internet
Alphabetical Authors

Writing Basics 18

Use Your Own Words   Punctuation
Writing Note Cards   Fact Versus Opinion
Identifying Complete Sentences   Your Own Facts and Opinions
Writing Complete Sentences   What's the Main Idea?
Proper Nouns

Writing the Report 27

Creating Categories   Writing the Title Page and Bibliography
Report-Planning Chart   Editing Marks
Writing the Introduction   Spelling Counts
Writing the Conclusion   What Do You Think?

Report Pizzazz 38

Adding a Computer Graphic: *Kid Pix*®   The Research Poster
Adding a Computer Graphic: Make a Multimedia Presentation:
ClarisWorks®   *HyperStudio*®
Report Projects   Planning an Oral Presentation
Make Appropriate Illustrations

Final Checklist 46

Resources 47

Answer Key 48

Introduction

Writing research reports can prove to be an enjoyable experience for your children. *How to Write a Simple Report* takes children through the basic steps necessary to bring a topic through all the "work-in-progress" stages—from researching through the final presentation. In the end, your children are sure to think that report writing is fun and exciting.

This book is divided into the following sections:

Getting Started

Your students will learn what a research report is and have the opportunity to see the report-writing process modeled by writing a class report. They will select and narrow a topic and ask the important questions: Who? What? When? Where? Why? and How?

Using the Library

Children will explore the library, and learn to use the Dewey Decimal System, computerized library search programs, encyclopedias, and computer and CD-ROM resources.

Writing Basics

In this section, your children will practice the basics needed to write a quality report. They will have the opportunity to practice writing facts in their own words, write note cards, identify and write complete sentences, use correct capitalization and punctuation, and more.

Writing the Report

Your children will put their reports together by creating categories, sequencing facts, writing introductory and concluding paragraphs, adding the title page and bibliography, and editing.

Report Pizzazz

Students will learn to creatively enhance a report with auditory, visual, and tactile products that will clarify and add sparkle to their presentations.

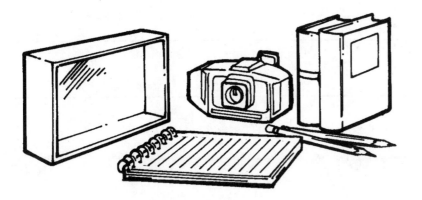

What is a Report?

A report presents information that you have learned about a topic. You can use books, encyclopedias, CD-ROM programs, and even Internet resources. After collecting interesting information, write about the things you have learned.

Choosing a topic is where you begin. Select a topic that interests you. Read the topics in the box below to help you or choose a topic of your own.

dogs	trains	pollution	lions
cars	hampsters	elephants	butterflies
cats	bats	weather	whales
airplanes	recycling	bears	silkworms
hamsters	penguins	ants	soccer

On the lines below, write three topics that interest you.

Favorite Topics

1. _____

2 _____

3. _____

Write a Class Report

Your children will understand the report-writing process much better if it can be modeled while writing a group report. While each step of this process is explained in detail in the pages of this book, here is an overview of the steps that you and your children can participate in together. The class report should last for the duration of your report-writing unit. Before asking the children to complete a new task, model that task as a group with the class report. Your children will experience greater success with their own reports when they are able to see the class report come together.

Developing the Topic

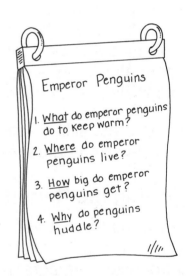

Begin by deciding on a topic as a group. Then ask the children to get specific and think about how they can narrow the topic to make it easier to research. For example, rather than researching penguins, narrow the topic to emperor penguins. Next, ask the children what things they would like to learn about the topic. List their questions on chart paper. Encourage them to use the five Ws in creating their questions. Incorporate skill practice with pages 8–10 as the children work on their individual reports.

Emperor Penguins

1. What do emperor penguins do to keep warm?

2. Where do emperor penguins live?

3. How big do emperor penguins get?

4. Why do penguins huddle?

Using the Library

Model the use of the card catalog or computer catalog for your students. Search for several nonfiction books, record the call numbers, and then find them on the library shelves. Demonstrate how to locate additional information in encyclopedias, on CD-ROM encyclopedias, and on the Internet. Display the books and articles on a table in your classroom. Incorporate skill practice with pages 11–17 as the children work on their individual reports.

Gathering Facts and Taking Notes

Each day, read a few pages of factual information about the chosen topic to your children. Invite them to raise their hands when they hear interesting facts. Ask the children to say the facts in their own words and then write the facts on giant note cards made from 9" x 12" (23 cm x 33 cm) sheets of construction paper. Incorporate skill practice with pages 18 and 19 as children work on their individual reports.

Write a Class Report *(cont.)*

Categorizing and Sequencing Information

After you have gathered a large assortment of factual information, begin to review it and decide on categories that have emerged from the research. Ask the children to name three or four categories as you write each one on a different sheet of chart paper. Read each note card aloud to the class and have them decide under which category the fact belongs.

Draw the children's attention to the order of the facts in each category. The facts in each category can later be sequenced for better understanding and smooth reading. Are the facts in logical sequence? Does the category need more information? As a class, sequence the facts and add information as needed.

Ant Homes
1. Ants live in colonies.
2. Some ants build mounds.

Ants Are Insects
1. Ants can be black, brown, red, or blue.
2. Ants have three body parts.

Incorporate skill practice in the writing basics on page 20–26 and preliminary report writing on pages 27–28 as the children work on their individual reports.

Writing the Report

Once the facts have been gathered, categorized, and sequenced, it's time to write the report. Discuss with your children and model how to write an introductory paragraph. Add the factual information that was previously placed in categories. Then write a group conclusion.

Continue to incorporate report-writing skills using pages 29–32 as the children work on their individual reports.

Adding a Title Page and Bibliography

Finally, you will add a title page and a bibliography to your report. Model for the children how to neatly write the title page, including all necessary information.

The bibliography will be a bit more difficult to write. Using a nonfiction book and an encyclopedia, show the children where the author's name and publisher information can be found. Then demonstrate how this information is ordered and how punctuation is used in writing the bibliography.

Use page 31 to assist children in writing their own title pages and bibliographies.

Write a Class Report *(cont.)*

Editing the Report

Since the class report will actually be handwritten by you, it is likely that not much editing will be needed. If this is the case, write an excerpt from the class report on the board and include a variety of mistakes such as spelling, capitalization, punctuation, run-on sentences, etc. Ask the children to identify each mistake and write the corresponding editing mark beside it. You may also want to display an error-filled excerpt with editing marks already marked. Ask the children to tell what each editing mark means and what needs to be done to the writing to correct it.

Incorporate pages 32–37 to help children as they work on their individual reports.

Adding Pizzazz!

Pages 38–46 provide ideas and instructions for creating projects, illustrations, multimedia presentations, and more to enhance the final report. A class report lends itself to the use of many of these activities. Explain the different types of projects to your children and allow them to choose the ones they would like to create. Encourage children to work with partners to create their posters, displays, and computer programs. The success the children experience by working with their classmates will encourage them to include creative additions to their individual reports.

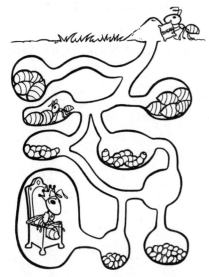

Let's Get Specific!

Your next step is to narrow your topic. When you narrow your topic, you choose a smaller subject to write about.

Here are some examples.

Topic	Narrowed Topic
dogs	beagles
desert	saguaro cactus
bats	fruit bats

Now it's your turn. Read each topic below. Then write a narrowed topic on the line beside it.

Topic	Narrowed Topic
ocean animals	_____
birds	_____
insects	_____
sports	_____

Write your topic below. Think about how you want to narrow your topic and write it on the line.

My Topic   **My Narrowed Topic**

_____   _____

Thinking About Your Topic

Before you get started it is important to think about the things you want to learn about your topic. You will find lots of information about the topic. Now you need to decide what you want to learn.

Here is an example:

My topic is fruit bats.

1. Where do they live?
2. What do they eat?
3. How big are they?
4. How big are their babies?
5. How do they hang upside down?

Write the name of your topic. Then write several questions that you have about your topic.

My topic is_____

My questions:

1. _____

2. _____

3. _____

4. _____

5. _____

The Five Ws

Before you begin your research, think about some questions that you would like to answer. It is helpful to use the five Ws (*who*, *what*, *where*, *when*, and *why*).

Use each word below to begin a question about your topic.

Who _____

_____

What _____

_____

Where _____

_____

When _____

_____

Why _____

_____

Write one more question using the word *how.*

How _____

_____

The Dewey Decimal System

All the nonfiction books in the library are arranged according to a number system called the Dewey Decimal System, created by a famous librarian named Melvil Dewey. It has 10 major divisions from 000 for General Works to the 900s for History. Each major division is divided into 10 parts, each focusing on one aspect of the category. Each subdivision is again divided into 10 sections. Each book has its own call number, indicating its category, to help find it easily on the shelves. In many libraries this information is found on a computer system.

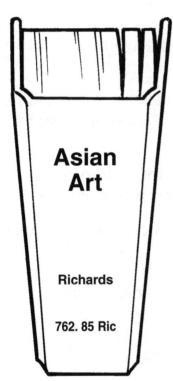

Asian Art

Richards

762. 85 Ric

The Dewey Decimal System

000–099	General Works (encyclopedias, atlases)
100–199	Philosophy (philosophy, psychology)
200–299	Religion (religions, mythology)
300–399	Social Science (law, government)
400–499	Language (languages, dictionaries)
500–599	Pure Sciences (math, biology, space)
600–699	Applied Sciences and Useful Arts (business, farming, cooking, cosmetology)
700–799	Fine Arts (music, sports, art, photography)
800–899	Literature (poetry, plays)
900–999	History (travel, biography, geography)

The Card Catalog

Some libraries use card catalogs to list the books on the library shelves. A card catalog has drawers of cards which index the books by author, subject, and title. The cards are arranged in alphabetical order in each category. The label on the front of each drawer tells the first and last cards in that drawer. Once you have found a book listed in the card catalog, a call number indicates where the book can be found on the library shelves.

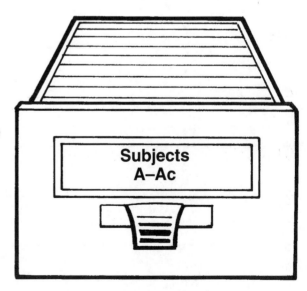

Subjects
A–Ac

Searching for Books

Most libraries have computer search programs to help you find the books you need. Follow the instructions below to find books about your topic.

(Teacher Note: Instructions may vary, depending on the search program at your school.)

1. From the main menu, click on **Subject.**

2. Type the name of your topic and then press the **Return** key. A list of subjects will appear on the screen.

3. Click on a selection of **Nonfiction Books** about your topic. A list of nonfiction books about your topic will appear.

4. Beside each title, you will see a call number. The call number is the number you will use to find your book. Some programs also show whether the book is IN or OUT of the library.

5. Write down the title and call number for each book that interests you, or double-click on the book title to get more information about the book.

6. To do another subject search, click on the **Close** button at the bottom of the screen, and then begin again.

Keep track of the books you find on the computer on the lines below.

        Call Number   **Title**

_____

_____

_____

_____

_____

Finding Books on Library Shelves

All nonfiction books are arranged on the shelves by their numbers. The numbers become larger as you move to the right on a shelf. See the shelves below for an example.

shelf 1

shelf 2

Look at the call numbers below. Write the shelf number and shelf position (beginning, middle, or end) where the book is found. The first one has been done for you.

	Shelf	**Shelf Position**
1. **513**	shelf 1	end
2. **039**		
3. **982**		
4. **734**		
5. **211**		
6. **658**		
7. **325**		
8. **691**		

Alphabetical Authors

Many books have the same call numbers. You will find these books together on a library shelf. Books with the same call number are arranged in alphabetical order, using the first three letters of the author's last name. See the shelf below for an example.

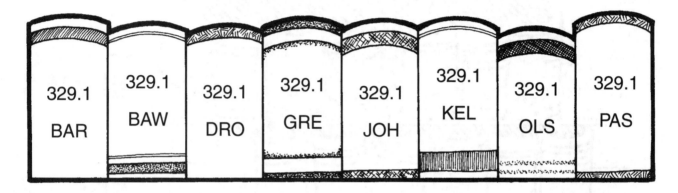

Below, you will see the first three letters of several authors' last names. Write them on the books in the correct order.

(**Hint:** If the first letter is the same, you need to use the second letter to determine the order.)

BRO	VAN	KEL	MUN
SPI	HUT	MEY	KEA

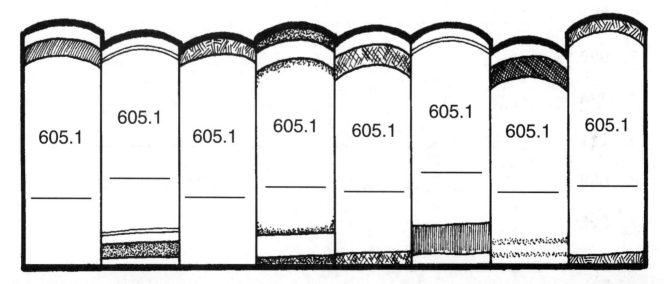

Where Can I Find It?

To use an encyclopedia, select the volume that begins with the first letter of your topic. Once you have the volume you need, it's time to find your topic.

The next step is to decide whether your topic will be at the beginning, middle, or end of the encyclopedia. You will need to look at the *second* letter of your topic to decide.

The beginning of the encyclopedia: letters a, b, c, d, e, f, g, h, i

The middle of the encyclopedia: letters j, k, l, m, n, o, p, q

The end of the encyclopedia: letters r, s, t, u, v, w, x, y, z

Read the words below. Write the encyclopedia volume and location for each word. The first one has been done for you.

	Volume	**Location**
car	volume C	beginning
dog		
hamster		
weather		
trains		

Write the encyclopedia volumes and locations for your topic.

My topic is _____.

Volume	**Location**

Using a CD-ROM Encyclopedia®

Teacher Note: These instructions accompany *Microsoft Encarta 97 Encyclopedia.* You can modify these instructions for the CD-ROM encyclopedia program that you have.

Searching for information about your topic is very easy using a CD-ROM encyclopedia program like *Microsoft Encarta 97 Encyclopedia.* Once the program is on your computer screen, follow these instructions to find an article about your topic.

1. On the home screen, click on **Encyclopedia Articles.**

2. Click on **Find** at the top of the screen. A search window will appear.

3. Click on the **Search** window and then type in the name of your topic.

4. A list of topics will appear on the window. Click on the topic of your choice. You will need to select the article carefully. For example, if you type the word **cat,** you will see several topics including Cat Family; CAT Scanner; and Cat, Domestic.

5. Click on the topic of your choice.

6. Read the article to find information for your report. It may be helpful for you to print the article or a section of the article. Follow these instructions for printing.

   a. To print the whole article, go to the **File** menu at the top of the screen and drag to **Print**. A print window will appear.

   b. Click on **Print.** Another print window will appear.

   c. Click on **Print** again. Your article will begin to print.

   d. To print only a section of the article, highlight the article by clicking and dragging over the selected information. Then follow steps **b** and **c** above to print the information.

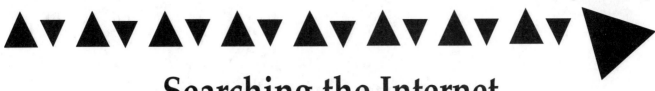

Searching the Internet

You can search the Web to find additional information on a variety of Web sites. To do an Internet search, follow the directions below.

1. Access the World Wide Web and then type in one of the search engines listed at the bottom of this page.

2. In the **search window**, type a few words relating to your topic. Here are some examples:

beagles AND behavior
desert AND animals
weather AND tornadoes

3. A list of articles will appear. Click on an article to find information about your topic.

Internet Search Engines

Yahooligans!
http://www.yahooligans.com/

Lycos
http://www.lycos.com/

Yahoo
http://www.yahoo.com/

WebCrawler
http://www.WebCrawler.com/

Excite
http://www.excite.com/

Alta Vista Technology, Inc.
http://www.altavista.com/

> **Teacher Note:** To ensure the safety of your students, closely monitor Internet use.

Use Your Own Words

When you write a report, it is important to use your own words. This means that you cannot copy sentences exactly as they are written in your sources. Read each set of sentences below. Write the same information using your own words. The first one has been done for you.

1. Cats learn through observation. A mother cat teaches her kittens how to hunt, catch prey, and use a litter box.

> **My own words:**
>
> *Kittens learn from their mothers. The mother shows the kittens how to use a litter box, hunt, and catch prey.*

2. The Grand Canyon is extremely beautiful, containing towering buttes, mesas, and valleys within its main gorge.

My own words:

_____

_____

3. The elephant is the largest living land mammal.

My own words:

_____

_____

4. Hailstones contain clusters of raindrops that have collided and frozen together.

My own words:

_____

_____

Writing Note Cards

As you research your topic, you will need to write each fact on a different 3" x 5" (8 cm x 13 cm) note card. Write the name of your source and the page number where it was found at the top of the card. Then write the fact on the card in your own words. Look at the examples below.

Giraffes by J. Jones
p. 11

A giraffe has a very long tongue.

Giraffes by J. Jones
p. 15

A giraffe's tongue can wrap around your waist.

Now read the following paragraph from a nonfiction book and write a fact on the index card below.

Giraffes are the tallest of all animals. They can grow to be 18 feet high. Giraffes usually have three horns on their heads. Dark patches on their coats help to camouflage them in the shade of trees.

Be sure to keep your index cards in a stack and hold them together with a rubber band.

Identifying Complete Sentences

When you write a report, it is important to write complete sentences. A complete sentence tells *who* or *what* (noun), and it tells *what happened* (verb).

Read each line below. Write **yes** if it is a complete sentence and **no** if it is an incomplete sentence. If it is a complete sentence, add the proper capitalization and punctuation.

_____ 1. a puppy should be carried properly

_____ 2. fog is a cloud that touches the ground

_____ 3. the sharp teeth of the shark

_____ 4. cats see well at night

_____ 5. soccer is played by men, women, and children

_____ 6. checkups for dogs

_____ 7. the body of an airplane

_____ 8. a dolphin is a kind of whale

_____ 9. strong wind storms

_____ 10. most desert mammals are nocturnal

_____ 11. the largest shark is the whale shark

_____ 12. two baseball teams

_____ 13. crops can grow in the desert

_____ 14. hunting at night

Writing Complete Sentences

Below is a series of incomplete sentences. Use each phrase to write a complete sentence.

1. fluffy cumulus clouds

   _____

2. short-haired or long-haired dogs

   _____

3. a fast train

   _____

4. stripes on a zebra

   _____

5. rain, snow, hail, and sleet

   _____

6. fish in the ocean

   _____

7. long cactus needles

   _____

8. visits to the veterinarian

   _____

Proper Nouns

Capital letters belong in places in addition to the beginnings of sentences. The proper names of people, places, and things are also capitalized.

Here are some examples.

Many bats live in **N**ew **M**exico.
Carlsbad **C**averns is a cave where many bats live.

Read the sentences below. Show each letter that should be capitalized by writing a capital letter above it. Then rewrite the sentences correctly.

1. The grand canyon is in arizona.

   _____

2. The colorado river flows through the grand canyon.

   _____

   _____

3. Grasslands can be found in north america, in south america, and in south africa.

   _____

   _____

4. The navajo people live in arizona, new mexico, and utah.

   _____

   _____

5. The indian elephant lives in india and other parts of asia.

   _____

   _____

Punctuation

When writing your report, you must be sure to use the correct punctuation mark at the end of each sentence.

A *telling sentence* needs a period.

An *asking sentence* needs a question mark.

Use the correct punctuation at the end of each sentence.

1. Cats are interesting animals
2. Did you know that there are 1,000 kinds of bats
3. Have you ever wondered how a polar bear keeps warm
4. The blue whale is the largest of all whales
5. This report is about trains
6. What is your favorite kind of animal
7. Do you have a pet dog
8. Many animals live in the ocean
9. My favorite sport is baseball
10. Spiders are not insects
11. Have you ever seen an ant farm
12. Many kinds of birds live in the rain forest

On the lines below, write a telling sentence and an asking sentence about your topic.

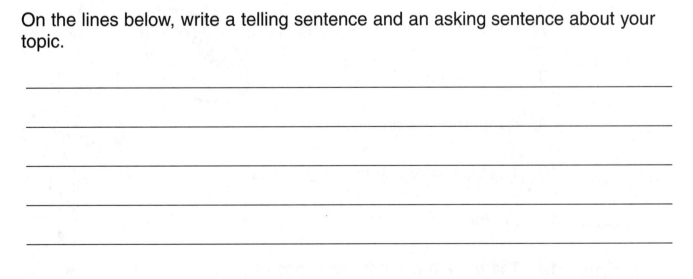

_____

_____

_____

_____

_____

Fact Versus Opinion

A **fact** is something that is true.

Example: There are many breeds of cats.

An **opinion** is how you feel about something.

Example: Cats are cute.

Read each sentence below. If the sentence is a fact, write an **F** on the line. If the sentence is an opinion, write an **O** on the line.

_____ 1. Dogs are great pets.

_____ 2. Sharks are cool.

_____ 3. There are many different kinds of ocean animals.

_____ 4. Rattlesnakes are reptiles.

_____ 5. A black widow spider is poisonous.

_____ 6. Soccer is a popular sport in many parts of the world.

_____ 7. Football is the most exciting sport.

_____ 8. Giraffes live in Africa.

_____ 9. Kangaroo rats are cute.

_____ 10. The blue whale is the largest whale.

_____ 11. Scorpions are scary.

_____ 12. There are many different kinds of ants.

Your Own Facts and Opinions

You probably have many opinions about your topic, but your report will contain mostly facts about the topic. You can use facts to show the reader your opinions. Read the examples below.

Opinion: Fruit bats are cute.

Facts: The face of a fruit bat looks like a fox.
Fruit bats are called flying foxes.
A fruit bat has big, round eyes.

Opinion: The fruit bat is an interesting animal.

Facts: A fruit bat carries her baby with her when she flies.
A fruit bat can have a six-foot wingspan.
Fruit bats are not blind. They use their eyesight to see in the dark.

On the lines below, write two of your opinions about your topic. Then, for each opinion, write a few facts to support it.

Opinion: _____

Facts: _____

_____

_____

Opinion: _____

Facts: _____

_____

_____

What's the Main Idea?

A main idea sentence tells about the things that will be written in a paragraph. Read each paragraph below. Choose the correct main-idea sentence from the bottom of the page. Then cut and glue the sentence above the paragraph.

1. They need to have regular visits to the veterinarian. They also need good food and plenty of exercise.

2. Many of them have good eyesight. Fruit bats use their eyesight to guide them when they fly at night.

3. Clams, crabs, and sea urchins live on the ocean floor. Many colorful fish swim in the ocean. Mammals, such as whales and seals, also live there.

4. The owner must work with the dog every day to train it. Offering treats can be helpful in training. It is most important for the dog to receive love and praise.

5. They sleep in caves, trees, and barns during the day. At night, they wake up and hunt for food in the dark.

6. Even though they live in water, they breathe air. They do not lay eggs. Their babies are born alive.

Bats are nocturnal animals.	Many creatures live in the ocean.
Whales are mammals.	Dogs need to have proper care.
Training a dog takes time.	Bats are not blind.

Creating Categories

It's time to look at your note cards and separate the facts into categories. See the example below.

Topic: Hammerhead Sharks

Category 1: How they look

Category 2: Where they live

Category 3: What they eat

Hammerhead Sharks

Hammerheads live in warm waters.

Hammerhead Sharks

The eyes and nostrils are at the ends of their heads.

Write the name of your topic below. Then write three or four categories for the facts you have gathered.

Topic: _____

_____

Category 1: _____

_____

Category 2: _____

_____

Category 3: _____

_____

Category 4 (optional): _____

_____

Note: Keep the cards for each category together and use a rubber band to hold them in place.

Report-Planning Chart

You have gathered all of your information. You have separated the information into categories. Now use this chart to begin writing the body of your report.

Facts for the First Category

_____

_____

_____

_____

Facts for the Second Category

_____

_____

_____

_____

Facts for the Third Category

_____

_____

_____

_____

Writing the Introduction

The introduction is an important part of a report. The introductory paragraph tells the reader about what is coming up in the report. Look at the categories that you have created for your report. Think of an interesting main idea sentence and then write the introduction by mentioning each category in the order it will appear in the report.

See the example below of a report with a topic and three categories. Then read the introductory paragraph that discusses these categories.

Topic: Blue Whale

Categories:
1. How the blue whale looks
2. Where the blue whale lives
3. Blue whale families

Introductory paragraph:

How much do you know about the blue whale? They are very interesting animals. This report will tell about what the blue whale looks like. It will also tell about where the blue whale lives and interesting things about how blue whales take care of their families.

Now it's your turn. Write your *main-idea* sentence:

_____

_____

Write a sentence about each category that will be in your report.

_____

_____

_____

Writing the Conclusion

The conclusion is a summary of what you have written about in your report. There are many things that you can include in your conclusion. Read the list below to get some ideas.

> - A summary of your main points
> - Your opinion about your research
> - What you learned from writing the report
> - Why the subject is important to you
> - Where the reader can find more information about the topic

Read the concluding paragraphs below. Check the list above to see if any of the elements have been included. If you think it is a good concluding paragraph, write **yes** on the line. If it is not a good concluding paragraph, write **no** on the line.

_____ 1. Now you know all about rabbits. The end.

_____ 2. From this report, you have learned many interesting facts about seahorses. Now you know how they look, how they swim, and how they carry their babies. I enjoyed doing research about these amazing animals.

_____ 3. This is the end of my report. Good-bye!

_____ 4. There are many things to learn about the desert. It is filled with interesting plants and animals. After doing this research, I hope I will be able to visit the desert someday.

Writing the Title Page and Bibliography

Now it's time to add the finishing touches to your report. You will need a title page to place at the beginning of your report. It will tell the reader what the report is about and who wrote it. Here is an example of a title page.

Polar Bears

by Keevan Schimmel
Ms. Novy's class
September 28, 1999

Practice writing your own title page.

_____

_____

_____

_____

You will also need a bibliography page to place at the end of the report. Make a list of all the books and encyclopedias you used for your report. Arrange the list of books in alphabetical order. Use the examples below to help you. On a separate sheet of paper, practice writing your bibliography.

Nonfiction Book:

Author (last name, first name). Title. Publisher, Date.

Example: Ahlstrom, Mark. The Polar Bear. Macmillan Child Group., 1986.

Encyclopedia:

Encyclopedia. Volume. Publisher, Date.

Example: World Book Encyclopedia. Volume 7, World Book, Inc., 1993.

Editing Marks

Your teacher may edit your paper, or you may be asked to edit the paper yourself or with a partner. Use the editing marks below to help you. Be sure to check for each of the common errors listed, and make the corrections with a colored marker on your rough draft.

Editing your report may take more than one writing session to complete. Cut out and staple the checklist at the bottom of the page to your rough draft. As you edit for each common error, make a check in the corresponding box.

Add a period.	⊙	The bat flew into the cave⊙
Add a comma.	⌃	He ate carrots⌃ apples, and crackers.
Capitalize the letter.	≡	S̲am is nine today.
Spell the word correctly.	SP	Jumf as high as you can. Jump
Use a lowercase letter.	lc	Today is his Birthday! birthday
Begin a new paragraph.	¶	I have a dog for a pet. His name is Duke. He is brown and has big eyes. I also have a cat. Her name is Daisy. She is orange and has sharp claws.

CUT HERE

- -

Rough-Draft Checklist

☐ Periods   ⊙   ☐ Spelling   SP

☐ Commas   ⌃   ☐ Lowercase letters   lc

☐ Capitals   ≡   ☐ Appropriate paragraphs ¶

Spelling Counts

Teacher Note: High-frequency words are words that are used often in writing. Your children can easily check the spelling in their reports by using this booklet of high-frequency words.

Duplicate pages 33–36 for each child. To assemble the booklet, cut apart the pages, stack them in sequence and staple them together.

My Book of Words

A

about
after
all
am
an
and
are
as
at

_____
_____
_____
_____
_____
_____

B

back
be
because
been
big
but
by

_____
_____
_____
_____
_____
_____

C

came
can
come
could
_____

_____
_____
_____

_____

_____

_____

D

day
did
do
down

_____

_____

_____

E

_____

_____

_____

_____

_____

Spelling Counts *(cont.)*

F

first
for
from

_____

_____

_____

_____

G

get
go
going
got

_____

_____

_____

_____

H

had
has
have
he
her
here
him
his

_____

_____

_____

_____

_____

_____

_____

I

if
into
is
it

_____

_____

_____

_____

J

just

_____

_____

_____

_____

_____

_____

K

_____

_____

_____

_____

_____

_____

L

like
little
look

_____

_____

_____

_____

34

Spelling Counts *(cont.)*

M

made
make
me
more
my

_____
_____
_____
_____

N

no
not
now

_____
_____
_____
_____

O

of
off
on
one
only
or
our
out
over

_____
_____
_____
_____
_____
_____
_____

P

_____
_____
_____
_____

Q

_____
_____
_____

R

_____
_____
_____
_____
_____
_____

S

said
saw
see
she
so
some

_____
_____
_____

_____
_____
_____
_____
_____
_____
_____

Spelling Counts *(cont.)*

T _____

that _____
the _____
their _____
them _____
then _____
there _____
they _____
this _____
to _____
two _____

U

up _____

_____

_____

_____

_____

_____

V

very _____

_____

_____

_____

_____

_____

W _____
was
we _____
well
went _____
were
what _____
when
where _____
which
who _____
will
with _____
would

X

_____

_____

_____

Z

_____

_____

_____

Y _____

you _____
your

_____

_____

What Do You Think?

This is your chance to read a classmate's report. Your comments will help your classmate to improve his or her report. Answer the questions below.

1. Who wrote the report? _____

2. What is the name of the report?

   _____

3. Was the report easy to understand? Explain.

   _____

   _____

4. What did you learn from the report?

   _____

   _____

5. What did you think was interesting about the report?

   _____

   _____

6. Did you find any spelling or punctuation mistakes? Explain.

   _____

   _____

7. Write your suggestions and compliments about this report.

   _____

   _____

   _____

Adding a Computer Graphic:
KidPix®

Teacher Note: Use these instructions to direct your children in making computer graphics. These instructions have been created using *KidPix*. By modifying them, another drawing and painting program can be used in its place.

Step 1: Choose an appropriate illustration.

Think about the report you have written. You will want to make an illustration that helps the reader understand more about your topic.

Step 2: Create the picture.

Begin drawing your picture using the following directions.

- Select the **Pencil** tool and the desired color from the tool bar.
- Choose a line thickness and pattern from the **Options** bar below the picture.
- In addition to the pencil, you may want to use the paintbrush in creating your picture. Select the **Paintbrush** from the tool bar and then select a painting style from the options bar below.

Step 3: Add text to the picture.

To add text to the picture, select the **Typewriter** tool. Click on the screen to place the cursor in the desired location. From the tool bar, select the desired text color. Then type a sentence or two to accompany the picture. If more than one line is needed for the text, it is necessary to press the **Return** key on the keyboard. Unlike a typical word processing document, the text will not automatically shift to the next line. If you should happen to type beyond the screen, simply press the **Delete** key on the keyboard until the cursor can be seen again; then press the **Return** key to move to the next line.

Step 4: Save and print.

Go to the **File** menu and **Save** the document. Then select **Print** from the **File** menu.

Reminder: Any procedure can be removed by immediately selecting the **Undo Guy** from the tool bar.

Adding a Computer Graphic:
ClarisWorks®

Teacher Note: These instructions have been created using *ClarisWorks*. If properly modified, another word-processing clip-art program can be used in its place.

Step 1: Type the report.

Use these instructions to type your report in *ClarisWorks*.

- Open the *ClarisWorks* program.
- From the resulting window, select **Word Processing** and click **OK**.
- Then type the report.

Step 2: Add a clip-art graphic.

- Go to the **File** menu and drag the cursor to **Library**. Then drag to the desired library. A small window listing several graphics will appear on the screen.
- Move the cursor to the position where you want the graphic to appear.
- Click once on the name of a graphic in the list and a preview picture will appear on the window. Select the first graphic to be used in the project and then click on **Use**. The graphic will appear on your report.
- Adjust the size of the graphic by highlighting the graphic. To do this, click on the image once so that a small, dark square appears in each corner. Then click on the lower right square and drag to create the desired size.
- Move the graphic by clicking in the center of the image and dragging it to the desired location.

Step 3: Save and print.

Using the **File** menu, select **Save**. Then select **Print** from the **File** menu.

Report Projects

Adding pizzazz to your report is easy and fun with a project about your topic. Here are some great ideas that you can use to make eye-catching displays.

Dazzling Diorama

A **diorama** is a great way to display additional knowledge about your topic in an attractive way.

Materials

- 9-inch (22 cm) square of construction paper
- assorted construction-paper decorations
- crayons or markers
- scissors
- glue
- magazines

Directions

1. Begin by making a triangular stage from construction paper. Diagonally fold and crease a 9-inch (22 cm) square (Step 1).

2. Unfold the paper and, again, diagonally fold and crease the paper in the opposite direction (Step 2).

3. Open the square to reveal criss-crossed fold lines. Then cut along one of the fold lines, stopping at the center point (Step 3).

4. Spread glue on top of one of the cut triangular sections as shown (Step 4).

5. Place the opposite triangular section atop the glue-covered section, aligning the edges, and press them together (Step 5). You will now have a triangular stage for your diorama.

6. Color, cut out, and glue pictures to create a scene on your stage. Decorate your diorama.

Step 1

Step 2

Step 3

Step 4

Step 5

Picture Album

Some reports can be enhanced by an album of drawings or magazine cutouts. Add captions to each page.

Report Projects *(cont.)*

Newspaper Dough

This pliable dough is great for making durable models to accompany your report.

Materials

- newspaper strips
- water
- large bowl
- waxed paper
- flour
- tempera paint

Directions

1. Place newspaper strips in a large bowl of water. Allow the strips to soak overnight.

2. Pour out the water and squeeze the excess from the newspaper strips.

3. Make a doughy paste of flour and water. Add one cup of the paste to the newspaper strips.

4. Knead the paste and newspaper strips. Add more paste as needed and continue to knead the mixture until it makes a fairly smooth dough.

5. Mold the dough into the desired shape. Allow it to dry on waxed paper for a few days.

6. Paint the dried shape and allow it to dry before displaying.

Building with Boxes

Use cereal and cracker boxes, milk cartons, egg cartons, round oatmeal and chip containers, and more to make a variety of creations (town, rocket ship, robot, etc.).

Materials

- variety of empty containers
- scissors
- tempera paint
- glue
- dish soap
- paintbrush

Directions

1. Cut the boxes and cartons as desired to make the creation of your choice.

2. Glue the pieces together and allow the project to dry completely.

3. Add a few drops of dish soap to each color of tempera paint and mix. (The dish soap helps the paint to adhere to smooth surfaces and prevents cracking.)

4. Paint and decorate the project.

Make Appropriate Illustrations

Making illustrations will add interest to your report. Read your report and think about two or three facts that could be illustrated to help the reader better understand your topic.

Write two facts that could be illustrated. In the boxes, make simple sketches to illustrate your facts.

Fact: _____

_____

```



```

Fact: _____

_____

```



```

The Research Poster

A research poster is like a one-page report. The poster can include illustrations and plenty of factual information.

Materials

- a large poster board
- pencils
- glue
- samples from your research
- markers
- paints
- facts from your research

Directions

1. You will need to choose important facts about your topic to include on the research poster.

2. Decide what illustration you would like to draw on the poster. Sketch the drawing first on a large sheet of paper and place it on the poster to be sure that your drawing will be the right size. Begin your illustration by lightly drawing the outline in pencil. This will make erasing easier if you make a mistake.

3. Label the parts of your illustration, or write sentences below the illustration using facts from your research.

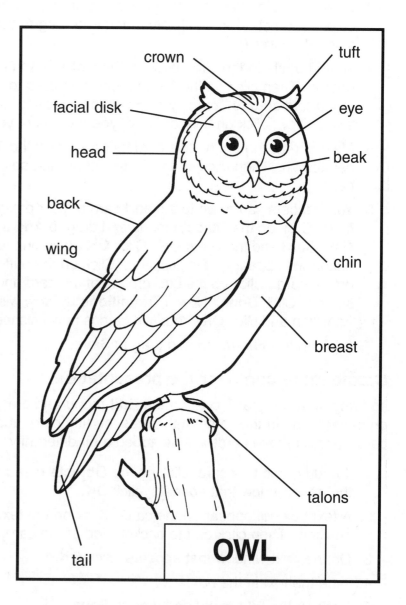

Make a Multimedia Presentation: *HyperStudio*®

You can give your report some zip by creating a multimedia computer presentation using *HyperStudio*. These instructions can be used with another multimedia program, if properly modified.

Create your title card.

1. Open the *HyperStudio* program. From the Home page, select **Create a New Stack.**

2. A window with instructions will appear. Click **OK.**

3. Make a colored background by clicking on the **Color** menu and dragging to the desired color. Then click on the **Tools** menu and drag to the paint can. Click on the card and the color will cover it.

4. To add a title to the card, click on the **Color** menu again and drag to the text color of your choice. Then click on the **Tools** menu and drag to **T** (text). Next, click on the **Options** menu and drag to **Text Style.** From the resulting window, select **24** from the list of text sizes. Now, click on the card and type the title of your report.

5. Make a drawing on the title card by clicking on the **Tools** menu and dragging to the paintbrush. Then click on the **Color** menu and select a color. Paint your picture on the card.

6. Your readers can move to the next card of your presentation if you add a button to the title card. Click on the **Objects** menu and drag to **Add a Button.** In the resulting window, type **Next Card** and then click **OK.** Click **OK** again on the next window that appears. The button will appear on the title card. Click on the button and drag it to the desired position on the card. Click on the background of the card and a new window will appear on the screen. Click **Done.** Now a **Transitions** window will appear on the screen. Select a transition and click **OK.** Your title card is now finished.

7. Click on the **File** menu and drag to **Save**.

Create more cards for the presentation.

To bring up a new card, click on the **Edit** menu and drag to **New Card**. The card will appear on the screen. In the same manner as the title card, add a background and a painting to each card. Text on these cards will be added a bit differently.

1. To add a text to a card, click on the **Objects** menu and drag to **Add a Text Object.** On the next window that appears, click **OK.**

2. A text box will appear on the card. Click on the text box and drag it to the desired position. Then click on the background of the card.

3. On the next window that appears, click **OK.**

4. Type the text in the box.

5. Click on the **File** menu and drag to **Save.**

Planning an Oral Presentation

Giving an oral presentation is a great way to share your research with several people at one time. This kind of presentation involves much more than just reading your report. Use this guide to plan an interesting presentation. You will write down the things you plan to say and then practice memorizing the script so you won't need to depend on it during the presentation.

1. Introduce yourself and your topic.

   _____

   _____

2. Tell about why you decided to research this topic.

   _____

   _____

3. Share a few interesting facts from each of your report paragraphs.

   _____

   _____

   _____

   _____

4. Show and explain a poster, illustration, or project that goes along with your report.

   _____

   _____

   _____

5. Share some of your opinions about your topic.

   _____

   _____

   _____

   _____

6. Ask your audience if they have any questions.

Final Checklist

It's time to take one last look at your report. Use this checklist to help you make your final corrections.

☐ Does the report look nice and neat?

☐ Is there a title page and a bibliography?

☐ Is my report clear? Does it make sense?

☐ Did a friend read it? Did he or she suggest changes?

☐ Do the paragraphs each begin with a topic sentence?

☐ Did I check for proper spelling?

☐ Did I check for proper capitalization and punctuation?

☐ Are appropriate illustrations included?

What do you think of your report? Write your comments below.

_____

_____

_____

_____

_____

Resources

Software

ClarisWorks® 4.0 (1995). Apple Corporation.

HyperStudio® (1996). Roger Wagner Publishing, Inc.

KidPix® (1994). The Learning Company.

Microsoft Encarta 97 Encyclopedia® (1993–1996). Microsoft Corporation.

Teacher Created Materials Resources

TCM 2182 *Kid Pix for Terrified Teachers.* Lifter, Marsha and Marian E. Adams. 1997.

TCM 2185 *ClarisWorks for Terrified Teachers.* Rosengart, Terry. 1999.

TCM 2332 *How to Write a Research Report*. Null, Kathleen Christopher. 1998.

Online Services

America Online (800) 827-6364

Compuserv (800) 848-8990

Netscape (800) 254-1900

Prodigy (800) 776-3449 ext. 629

Web Sites

Animal. http://www.discovery.com/cams/cams.html

Bill Nye, the Science Guy's Nye Labs Online. http://nyelabs.kcts.org/

The Bug Club. http://www.ex.ac.uk/bugclub/

Insect World. http://www.insect-world.com

Dan's Wild Wild Weather Page. http://www.whnt19.com/kidwx/

Earth Watch Weather on Demand. http://www.earthwatch.com/

O. Orkin Insect Zoo. http://www.orkin.com/html/o.orkin.html

Kennedy Space Center. http://www.ksc.nasa.gov

KidsHealth. http://kidshealth.org

MapQuest. http://www.mapquest.com

New England Aquarium. http://www.neaq.org

The Science Club. http://www.halcyon.com/sciclub/

Thinking Fountain. http://www.smm.org/sln/tf/n/

The "Weather Dude".® http://www.nwlink.com/~wxdude/

Answer Key

Page 13

2. Shelf #1   beginning
3. Shelf #2   end
4. Shelf #2   middle
5. Shelf #1   middle
6. Shelf #2   beginning
7. Shelf #1   middle
8. Shelf #2   beginning

Page 14

BRO
HUT
KEA
KEL
MEY
MUN
SPI
VAN

Page 15

2. dog   volume D   beginning
3. hamster   volume H   beginning
4. weather   volume W   end
5. trains   volume T   end

Page 20

1. yes   A puppy should be carried properly.
2. yes   Fog is a cloud that touches the ground.
3. no
4. yes   Cats see well at night.
5. yes   Soccer is played by men, women, and children.
6. no
7. no
8. yes   A dolphin is a kind of whale.
9. no
10. yes   Most desert mammals are nocturnal.
11. yes   The largest shark is the whale shark.
12. no
13. yes   Crops can grow in the desert.
14. no

Page 21

Accept reasonable responses.

Page 22

1. The Grand Canyon is in Arizona.
2. The Colorado River flows through the Grand Canyon.
3. Grasslands can be found in North America, in South America, and in South Africa
4. The Navajo people live in Arizona, New Mexico, and Utah.
5. The Indian elephant lives in India and other parts of Asia.

Page 23

1. Cats are interesting animals.
2. Did you know that there are 1,000 kinds of bats?
3. Have you ever wondered how a polar bear keeps warm?
4. The blue whale is the largest of all whales.
5. This report is about trains.
6. What is your favorite kind of animal?
7. Do you have a pet dog?
8. Many animals live in the ocean.
9. My favorite sport is baseball.
10. Spiders are not insects.
11. Have you ever seen an ant farm?
12. Many kinds of birds live in the rain forest.

Page 24

1. O
2. O
3. F
4. F
5. F
6. F
7. O
8. F
9. O
10. F
11. O
12. F

Page 26

1. Dogs need to have proper care.
2. Bats are not blind.
3. Many creatures live in the ocean.
4. Training a dog takes time.
5. Bats are nocturnal animals.
6. Whales are mammals.

Page 30

1. no
2. yes
3. no
4. yes